The Master Restorer

God Will Do It Again

Kenneth W. Hagin

Faith Library Publications®

Unless otherwise indicated, all scripture quotations are taken from the *New King James Version* of the Bible. Copyright © 1982 by Thomas Nelson. Used by permission. All rights reserved.

Scripture quotations marked AMP are taken from the *Amplified® Bible*, copyright © 2015 by the Lockman Foundation. Used by permission.

Scripture quotations marked AMPC are taken from the *Amplified® Bible, Classic Edition*, Copyright © 1954, 1958, 1962, 1964, 1965, 1987 by The Lockman Foundation. Used by permission.

Scripture quotations marked GW are taken from GOD'S WORD®, © 1995 *God's Word to the Nations*. Used by permission of Baker Publishing Group.

Scripture quotations marked GNT are from the *Good News Translation* in *Today's English Version-Second Edition*, Copyright © 1992 by American Bible Society. Used by Permission.

Scripture quotations marked MSG are taken from *The Message*. Copyright © 1993, 2002, 2018 by Eugene H. Peterson. Used by permission of NavPress. All rights reserved. Represented by Tyndale House Publisher, Inc.

Scripture quotations marked NLT are taken from the *Holy Bible, New Living Translation*, copyright © 1996, 2004, 2015 by Tyndale House Foundation. Used by permission of Tyndale House Publishers, Inc., Carol Stream, Illinois 60188. All rights reserved.

29 28 27 26 25 24 23   09 08 07 06 05 04 03

The Master Restorer: God Will Do It Again
ISBN-13: 978-0-89276-762-5
ISBN-10: 0-89276-762-6

Copyright © 2019 Rhema Bible Church
AKA Kenneth Hagin Ministries, Inc.
Printed in the USA

In the U.S. write:
Kenneth Hagin Ministries
P.O. Box 50126
Tulsa, OK 74150-0126
1-888-28-FAITH
rhema.org

In Canada write:
Kenneth Hagin Ministries of Canada
P.O. Box 335, Station D
Etobicoke (Toronto), Ontario
Canada M9A 4X3
1-866-70-RHEMA
rhemacanada.org

All rights reserved. Contents and/or cover may not be reproduced in whole or in part in any form without the express written consent of the Publisher. The Faith Shield is a trademark of Rhema Bible Church, AKA Kenneth Hagin Ministries, Inc., registered with the U.S. Patent and Trademark Office and, therefore, may not be duplicated.

Contents

Introduction 1

1. God Will Do It Again 5

2. Turnaround 19

3. Restored Twice 35

4. Moving Forward 53

Introduction

At the time of this writing, Rhema Bible Church was in the middle of renovations. It seemed an opportune time to express truths of spiritual restoration. I believe this book will encourage you greatly!

Many years ago, a pastor said to me, "I get a lot of visitors, but nobody wants to stay at the church." I had to be honest with him—the church needed a facelift. Weeds filled the front of the building, and leaves covered the entry area. The first thing that greeted a visitor when the doors opened was carpet that looked as though it were 100 years old! It was no wonder they stopped with just a visit.

Over time, things wear out. When carpet becomes worn and pews need to be repaired, it's time to renovate. When it is completed, a room or facility looks new. Our lives can experience something similar. We can become weary or stuck in the past and be in need of spiritual restoration. God wants us to live continually updated, refreshed, and restored!

As we renovated Rhema Bible Church, I thanked God for all the meetings held there. Praise God for what happened with my dad, the late Kenneth E. Hagin, during past *Winter Bible Seminars*. I thank the Lord for all the people who were healed on the pink line of carpet that used to be in the auditorium! Thank God for all the times the Holy Spirit moved. And yet, that all happened yesterday. We're here now.

Isaiah 43:18–19 says, *"Do not remember the former things, nor consider the things of old. Behold, I will do a new thing, now it shall spring forth."* I believe these verses are showing us that God wants to do something new in us. But first, we have to let go of the past.

Introduction

What is the "new thing" God wants to do in us? We find out as we walk with Him. In my heart, I feel there is more for the Body of Christ to do and more territory to take. God wants to take us to new heights and give us new plans and new levels of strength and power.

I believe the truths in this book will change your life. God is ready to do something new in you! He wants you to move forward with Him. He is the master restorer, and He is here to refresh and revive you.

1

God Will Do It Again

"I will give you back what you lost in the years when swarms of locusts ate your crops."

—Joel 2:25 (GNT)

Have you ever had to repair your car? They last a long time if you take care of them. But even with routine preventative maintenance, they can wear out. After my car reached 189,000 miles, the transmission decided it no longer wanted to operate, so I had it repaired.

What about your home? Have you ever renovated it? Afterward, everything is updated. Old things are removed. New things are brought in. Sometimes structural improvements and floor plan changes are made. Walls might come down and new ones built. It takes hard work and patience, but when it's done, your house is in brand-new condition.

Everything experiences wear and tear. Over time, things need to be replaced, updated, repaired, renovated, or restored. This is also true with spiritual things. Most Christians are filled with the Spirit after they accept Christ as their Savior. However, it is more than a one-time experience. Ephesians 5:18 tells us to *"be filled with the Spirit."* That word "be" means "be being." Verse 18 can, therefore, be read, "be being filled with the Spirit." In other words, we are to experience continual renewal. If we don't, we will dry up!

Refresh and Restore

It's easy to tell when Christians have "dried up" and need revival in their spiritual lives. They are no longer concerned about the lost, nor do they practice walking in love. Their joy seems to be gone. During a crisis, "faith words" are not spoken. The devil runs

God Will Do It Again

all over them, and they do nothing about it! When it comes to victory or what God did for them, they seem to only talk about the good old days.

Many people were filled with the Holy Spirit during the Charismatic Renewal in the 1970s and '80s. I have found that a lot of them are still "there" today. When Christians only talk about the golden days of yesteryear, they need to be spiritually revived. God did wonderful things in the past, and He will do it again today! Let's look at what the Bible says about times of restoration.

ACTS 3:19–21
19 Repent therefore and be converted, that your sins may be blotted out, so that times of refreshing may come from the presence of the Lord,
20 and that He may send Jesus Christ, who was preached to you before,
21 whom heaven must receive until the **times of restoration of all things**, which God has spoken by the mouth of all His holy prophets since the world began.

The Master Restorer: God Will Do It Again

According to these verses, God is saying that Jesus, will restore everything He promised to mankind. We tap into that when we repent and are converted to Christ. This passage also talks about times of refreshing. Notice the word "times" is not singular. It's plural, so it means more than once. *Times of refreshing* come from the presence of the Lord (v. 19), and verse 21 talks about times *of restoration* of all things. We need to expect continual refreshing and restoration. That's what the Holy Spirit wants to do in our lives!

Peter stated in these verses that refreshing and restoration would happen between Christ's ascension and His second coming. That means times of refreshing should occur throughout the church age until Jesus comes again. Whenever we talk about the "church," we are referring to the *ecclesia,* the called-out ones. That means *you and me.* This is supposed to be happening in our lives!

God Will Do It Again

We can rejoice in this! We are living at the right time to experience God's promise to refresh and restore us continually. He wants us to live the good life He designed. Jesus came to give us that new life, and the Holy Spirit refreshes it in us. Jesus brought salvation and restored righteousness. He brought healing and provision and came to restore what the enemy has stolen from us.

Everything God is doing in the earth since Jesus came is to further His plans of restoration. We play a part in it! God has a purpose for each of us to carry out while we are here. I want to challenge us all to expect times of refreshing and restoration with the Spirit of God continually.

Master Restorer

When we look in the Word, we see that God was always restoring, improving, repairing, and rebuilding throughout the Bible. In the Gospels, we see Jesus demonstrating God's willingness to restore people to health and wholeness, ultimately giving His life to restore mankind to God. Let's look at a few specific restorations.

God restored the earth. This will be a little theological, but stay with me! I want to show you how God is both a creator and a restorer.

GENESIS 1:1–3
1 In the beginning God created the heavens and the earth.
2 The earth was without form, and void; and darkness was on the face of the deep. And the Spirit of God was hovering over the face of the waters.
3 Then God said, "Let there be light"; and there was light.

God never created anything that wasn't perfect. Verse two, however, says the earth was without form and void. The Hebrew language gives the idea of a wasteland or ruin. How did it get that way?

Many theologians believe God kicked Satan and his cohorts out of Heaven. Jesus said in Luke 10:18, *"I saw Satan fall like lightning from heaven."* When the devil and demons fell to earth, it was so cataclysmic that it created the chaos we see in verse two. Scholars believe the rest of Genesis chapter 1 is God restoring the earth to what it was supposed to be. That is one perspective. I won't argue this belief one way or another, but it could explain how something God created perfectly became messed up!

In Genesis 1:2, the Holy Spirit hovered over that chaos. When God spoke, the Spirit of God was there to cause what was said to happen. Finally, in Genesis 1:31, God looked over everything He created or restored from the chaos, and said it was very good.

Don't get hung up on that theology. It's one explanation. There are several theological ideas. But realize that God is the creator *and* restorer. If He can fix something the size of this planet, He can certainly fix any situation for you! God is the master restorer. Nothing is too big for Him to repair!

The Master Restorer: God Will Do It Again

God restored Israel to their homeland. The Israelites had been taken into captivity by the Babylonians. It looked as though they would never go back home. But Daniel began to read Jeremiah's scrolls and prayed for the restoration of Israel. The angel Gabriel talked to him about the restoration and rebuilding of Jerusalem (Dan. 9:22–25). The Book of Nehemiah tells how the city walls of Jerusalem were rebuilt, and the Israelites' homeland was restored.

Jesus restored humanity to God. The Heavenly Father created mankind for Himself. He would come to the Garden of Eden to walk and talk with Adam. They shared a personal relationship. But Adam and his wife, Eve, sold out to the devil when they bought into the temptation to disobey God. Sin came, and they could no longer be in God's presence. Satan had stolen God's creation—mankind. But through Jesus Christ, we are restored spiritually. We can once again commune with our Heavenly Father.

God Will Do It Again

Now Is Your Time!

Remember the verses we started with in Acts 3:19–21? It says this restoration would continue to take place among God's people until Jesus returns. Let's look at this in *The Message* version: *"Now it's time to change your ways! Turn to face God so he can wipe away your sins, pour out showers of blessing to refresh you, and send you the Messiah he prepared for you, namely, Jesus. For the time being he must remain out of sight in heaven until everything is restored to order again just the way God, through the preaching of his holy prophets of old, said it would be."*

God wants to restore everything Satan has stolen from us. We can go through a lot in our lives—bad, tragic, and traumatic events happen to people. But we can put our trust in God. He will bring restoration.

JOEL 2:23–26

23 Be glad then, you children of Zion, and rejoice in the Lord your God; for He has given you the former rain faithfully, and

> He will cause the rain to come down for you—the former rain, and the latter rain in the first month.
>
> 24 The threshing floors shall be full of wheat, and the vats shall overflow with new wine and oil.
>
> 25 "So **I will restore to you** the years that the swarming locust has eaten, the crawling locust, the consuming locust, and the chewing locust, my great army which I sent among you.
>
> 26 You shall eat in plenty and be satisfied, and praise the name of the Lord your God, Who has dealt wondrously with you; and My people shall never be put to shame.

Everything will be restored! That is not only for the Israelites. If you are born again, then you are Abraham's seed and an heir to those promises (Gal. 3:29). We are adopted into the family, and therefore, we are the spiritual children of Zion (Rom. 8:12–17).

Whatever the devil has stolen, God's Word promises to restore. As we trust God and stand in faith, He will continue to work until

God Will Do It Again

His promises are fulfilled in our lives. We are His people. He deals wondrously with us and doesn't put us to shame. And if God ever fixed something once, He can fix it again!

God Will Do It Again

The devil may have brought chaos and messed up your life. You may feel ruined. Your heart may feel so shattered it looks unrepairable. But if you will commit your heart and life into the hands of the master restorer, He will put it back together again. When He's done, you won't even be able to tell it was broken!

God wants to come in and restore everything. He can repair *all* situations. He can even fix you! God has not forsaken you. He has not turned against you. If you have loved ones who have gone home to be with the Lord, He can restore your joy. No matter what has happened, know that God is there to refresh your life and bring restoration.

The Master Restorer: God Will Do It Again

If God restored in Bible days, He can do it again today. God will *always* make a way where there seems to be no way. Even when you think He could do no more, God will continue to rescue and restore again and again.

Restoration in Action

The master restorer is looking for messes He can fix, situations He can repair, lives He can put back together—things He can change just for you!

Don't let the devil tell you it's over. Maybe you were once close to God, but you're not where you used to be. You may feel as if you can never get back to that kind of relationship, but know that God can restore you! He is saying, *"If you come to me, I'll restore you. I'll put you back where you were."* This is your time to renew your relationship with Him.

If you are serving God but have lost your joy, that lets you know you need to be restored. We all need to be continually refreshed and refilled with the Holy Spirit every day. Read the

God Will Do It Again

Word. Pray in tongues. Fellowship with God. Let the Holy Spirit come in and refresh you with God's presence.

Pray this with me: *Heavenly Father, I thank You for sending Jesus to shed His blood on Calvary, to take stripes on His back for my healing, wipe away sin, defeat evil, and restore me to You. I ask You to restore the joy of my salvation and revive my life in You. Thank You for refreshing me with Your Presence. I put my life in Your hands, the master restorer, and I thank You for making all things new. In Jesus' Name, I pray. Amen.*

Scriptures to Review

1 Peter 3:18	**Psalm 51:12**
1 Peter 2:24	**Galatians 5:22**
1 John 3:5–8	**Psalm 16:11**

2

Turnaround

"When the enemy shall come in like a flood, the Spirit of the Lord will lift up a standard against him and put him to flight."

—Isaiah 59:19 (AMPC)

Nowadays it seems as though we have to see a specialist when something goes wrong. We used to take our cars to a general mechanic. Now we take it to a place that specializes in that particular car. We also have specialists in the medical field. A doctor often refers patients to a specialist for specific tests. It seems as if there are specialists in every field!

God is the turnaround specialist! When things went wrong for the people of God in the Bible, He repeatedly restored what their enemies had stolen. Sometimes the

The Master Restorer: God Will Do It Again

situation looked hopeless, but God turned it around. Not only is He the master restorer, but when it comes to turnarounds, there is no one greater than God.

The life of Joseph is one of the greatest turnaround stories in the Bible. It shows restoration, forgiveness, and impossible situations turned into supernatural promotion. I'll tell it in my own words, but you can read the entire story starting in Genesis 37.

Joseph was his father's favorite child. He wore a special coat given to him by his father. It was custom-made with many colors. His brothers hated him because he was the favorite. When Joseph began to have dreams from God, they hated him even more. In those dreams, God showed Joseph that his family would bow down to him. But nobody wanted to listen. They thought that bowing down to a teenager was ridiculous. Even Joseph's father rebuked him! (See Genesis 37:3–11.)

Turnaround

Joseph had mountaintop moments with God but encountered intense opposition from those closest to him. His brothers wanted to shut him down. Jacob probably thought his son's dreams were crazy. Joseph's brothers did not want the dreams to come true. They didn't believe him or even like him!

Maybe some of us have experienced situations like that. When we share what God told us, sometimes people come against us—even our families. They can't see God doing that, or they don't believe us. They have intense reactions, and we may find they act as if they don't even like us! Not everyone will believe in our dreams. The enemy will do whatever he can to keep us from experiencing what God has for us.

That's what happened to Joseph. The enemy tried to steal, kill, and destroy what God had for him. When Jacob sent Joseph to check on his brothers who were tending the flocks, they saw an opportunity to kill him! Ruben talked them out of murder, and they

The **Master Restorer:** God Will Do It Again

threw Joseph in an empty pit instead. While the brothers were eating, Ishmaelite traders approached. They realized they could make some money. So they sold Joseph as a slave, and he was taken to Egypt. His brothers took his coat, shredded it, and covered it with animal blood. They showed the coat to Jacob and told him a wild beast devoured Joseph. (See Genesis 37:12–36.)

In Genesis chapters 39 and 40, we see that Joseph was sold to Potiphar, a wealthy Egyptian, and how God's hand was upon him. Joseph was put in charge of his master's household until Potiphar's wife accused him of rape, and he was thrown into prison! But even there, God's hand was upon Joseph. The warden put Joseph in charge of all the prisoners. Eventually, Joseph interpreted dreams for Pharaoh's cupbearer and chief baker who were also in prison. The baker was executed, but the cupbearer was restored to serving the king. The cupbearer was supposed to speak on Joseph's behalf to Pharaoh. But once he was released from prison, he forgot.

Joseph couldn't seem to get a break. I imagine he wondered where God was in all this. He probably thought about his dreams and questioned if they would ever come to pass. In spite of what happened to him, Joseph was faithful to those over him and was promoted to prison leadership.

Enemy Attacks

Have you noticed that the enemy often attacks after a supernatural experience? The devil tries to steal from us immediately! One reason he strikes then is that our guard is usually down after a high point.

It's like winning a tough football game. Afterward, the coach has to say to the players, "That was a great win, but we have another game on Friday. Let's get with it!" After a big win, it's easy to lose the next game.

The Master Restorer: God Will Do It Again

Have you experienced that? A lot of us have been there. We're not ready for the fight because we are still rejoicing in our victory. I had one coach say, "Don't ever relax. Be ready to hit or be hit. I don't care if the whistle blows, and you're walking back to the huddle. Don't ever relax until you get in the huddle."

Having a supernatural experience with God doesn't mean everything is going to be great from that moment on. Some people will come against you. But don't get depressed, dejected, or disappointed. And don't give up. The devil may try to overwhelm us with a flood of circumstances. He will try to convince you that it's hopeless. Never believe his lies! Isaiah 59:19 says, *"When the enemy comes in like a flood, the Spirit of the Lord will lift up a standard against him."* God is on your side! He can turn any situation around.

God is looking for those who will cooperate with Him. As we trust Him, He will turn things around for us. We see it happen

Turnaround

throughout the Bible. Noah worked with God and built an ark. It saved his family, and two of every living creature. Gideon believed an angel and became the deliverer for Israel. David killed a giant and saved a nation.

Joseph cooperated with God and didn't give up. In tough situations, God gave him favor. He received favor in Potiphar's house, then in the jail, and even with Pharaoh. God continued to bless Joseph and kept turning his situations around.

If we will keep believing God and being faithful, it doesn't matter where we are or what happened. God will work through us. Even in dire circumstances, He will give us favor and bless us. Turnaround comes when we are willing to be faithful to God in the tough times.

God Turns the Tide

Joseph remained in prison for two years after the cupbearer promised to help him. Although he was over the prisoners, he was

The **Master Restorer:** God Will Do It Again

not free. His situation turned around in Genesis chapter 41. Pharaoh had a dream and did not know what it meant. None of his soothsayers or so-called "smart guys" were able to help. Finally, the cupbearer remembered Joseph and told Pharaoh, "There is a guy in the prison who interpreted my dream. I believe he can tell you what your dream means!"

They released Joseph from prison and brought him before Pharaoh. After hearing the dreams, Joseph immediately had the interpretation: there would be seven years of prosperity, followed by seven years of famine. Not only was Joseph able to tell Pharaoh what the dreams meant, but He also advised Pharaoh on what to do. The ruler of Egypt recognized Joseph's wisdom and intelligence. He placed Joseph in a position similar to a prime minister and gave him his signet ring! Joseph went from the prison to the palace in one day.

Turnaround

Now that Joseph was second in command in Egypt, things were looking up! As before, he remained faithful. In Genesis chapters 41 and 42, we see that he was in charge of the food program and saved a portion of the crops for seven years. When the famine hit, Joseph's storehouses were filled with more than enough food. People everywhere else were starving. When Joseph's father heard there was food in Egypt, he sent his sons to buy grain.

Joseph's brothers stood before him, but they didn't recognize him. He wasn't the kid they sold into slavery anymore! Can you imagine Joseph's thoughts when they bowed down to him? He didn't gloat over this, but he may have thought, "I told you so!"

Joseph didn't immediately tell them who he was. He played with them a little bit. He accused them of being spies. When he gave them sacks of grain, he held Simeon in prison and demanded that they return with

The Master Restorer: God Will Do It Again

Benjamin to verify their story. When the brothers returned to the land of Canaan, Jacob refused to send Benjamin. It was only after they ate all the grain that he relented.

When Joseph finally revealed his identity, he said to his brothers, *"But as for you, you meant evil against me; but God meant it for good, in order to bring it about as it is this day, to save many people alive"* (Gen. 50:20). The end of the story is great. Jacob and his family survived the famine and prospered for many years.

Joseph's brothers indeed wanted evil for him, but he forgave them. The devil wanted to destroy Joseph, but he remained faithful, and God turned every situation around for good.

Turnaround Specialist

The Bible is full of turnarounds. Abraham and Sarah couldn't have a son. But when God spoke, they believed—and kept believing for many years. God turned it around,

Turnaround

and they became parents (Gen. 21:7). Hezekiah was deathly sick, and the prophet told him he would die. He turned his face to the wall and prayed. God gave him 15 more years to live (2 Kings 20:1–7).

David returned to Ziklag with his men only to discover the city had been burned. Their wives and possessions were gone. But David encouraged himself (or you could say "renewed" himself) in the Lord. God turned it around, and they got everything back (1 Sam. 30:1–19).

In the New Testament, a man brought his epileptic son to Jesus. The disciples couldn't help the boy, but Jesus healed him (Matt. 17:14–18)! The lame man at the gate called Beautiful asked Peter and John for money. Peter was bold enough to say, "I don't have money for you, but I have something much better! Such as I have, I give to you." The man jumped to his feet and began to walk (Acts 3:1–8)!

The Master Restorer: God Will Do It Again

In most cases, God uses *people* to help turn situations around for others. Pharaoh turned Joseph's situation around, but God was behind it all. If we are open, He will use us to turn somebody else's situation around. When others help us, we sometimes do not realize that it's God turning things around. We look at the person and forget that God moved upon them to do so!

When it looks as though it's over and you're ready to quit, know that God will turn your situation around. He specializes in hopeless situations. If God turned it around for Joseph, He can turn it around for you.

When your life is a mess, He can restore it to order. When troubles are piled up higher than your head, God can set you on top of them. He can do the impossible. The turn-around specialist wants to work for you! He can reach to the lowest depths to fix your situation. He can go to the farthest place to restore you. He can restore what the enemy has taken from you.

Turnaround

Don't give up on God—He won't give up on you. He can turn your mess into a message. He can turn your test into a testimony. He can turn your trouble into triumph. This is your time! This is your hour to say, "All right God, I'm going to stay faithful to You, and I expect You to turn my situation around. I don't know how. I don't know when. But You can do it again!" Now begin to thank God because He's turning it around for you. He is the turnaround specialist!

Restoration in Action

Have you gone through situations where it looks as though you might be destroyed? Maybe you are in one of those situations right now. You are not alone! Don't think you're the only one. Many people have been through similar challenges—maybe worse. Know that God is with you. Keep trusting Him. Stay faithful. He *will* turn it around.

You may think your situation is impossible, but with God, *all* things are possible

The Master Restorer: God Will Do It Again

(Matt. 19:26)! Take a moment to turn your challenges over to God. Thank Him for your turnaround!

Pray this with me: *I thank You, Heavenly Father, for being my turnaround specialist. In the same way You fought for Joseph and brought him to where he needed to be, You're fighting for me. I put my life into Your hands. You're turning my situations around!*

Nothing is impossible with You. I look to You for help. I trust You to keep me from harm and watch over my life. I fix my eyes on You, not on what is temporary—and this situation is temporary!

You are my refuge and strength—an ever-present help in times of trouble. I can come boldly to You and find grace to help in time of need. Thank you for never abandoning me. I will not be frightened. I will be strong and courageous, for You are with me wherever I go.

God, You are the One Who saves me out of times of trouble. You restore health to me

Turnaround

and heal my wounds. Others have called me an outcast, and it seemed as though no one cared, but You bring restoration, multiplication, happiness, and thanksgiving!

Thank You, Jesus, for coming so I might have life and have it more abundantly. I know the devil only steals, kills, and destroys, but You are faithful to strengthen me and protect me from the evil one. No weapon formed against me will prosper! I bind the devil right now from operating in my life, and I loose God's ministering angels to work on my behalf.

Thank You, Lord, for turning my situation around!

Scriptures to Review

Luke 1:37	Hebrews 4:16
Psalm 46:1	2 Thessalonians 3:3
John 10:10	2 Corinthians 4:18
Hebrews 1:14	Psalm 94:14
Psalm 121:1–8	Isaiah 54:17

The Master Restorer: God Will Do It Again

Joshua 1:9   **Jeremiah 30:7, 17, 19**

Matthew 18:18–19

3

Restored Twice

"Come home, hope-filled prisoners! This very day I'm declaring a double bonus—everything you lost returned twice-over!"
—Zechariah 9:12 (MSG)

Have you ever tried to look into the future for a ray of hope? Just a glimpse of something that would help you to continue? Most of us have experienced what seemed like a long, hard road. We wondered if anything would ever change. One time, the Spirit of God rose in my spirit and said this during a service:

"Just keep on walking and keep on saying and keep on believing. Oh, there are a few more hurdles to pass. There are a few more rough spots to get over. But there will be victory in the end. Don't

The **Master Restorer**: God Will Do It Again

give up and don't despair, because if you do, the end will not be good. But if you will hold on, and if you will stay true to what you believe and say, you will see that the end will be great and there will cause for much rejoicing."

One of the oldest books in the Bible holds the story of a man who walked a hard road but held on, stayed true to what he believed, and saw a great victory in the end. That man is Job. He is misunderstood by many. But when we know the truth about Job, it will help us get through our troubles. Let's discover how God helped him in a mighty way.

The *New Living Translation* introduces Job this way: *"There once was a man named Job who lived in the land of Uz. He was blameless—a man of complete integrity. He feared God and stayed away from evil . . . He was, in fact, the richest person in that entire area"* (Job 1:1–3 NLT). *The Message* describes him as *"honest inside and out, a man of his word, . . . the most influential man in all the East!"*

Restored Twice

Job was a very wealthy man with a large family. God called him *"the finest man in all the earth"* (Job 1:8 NLT). The Bible says Satan, the Accuser, retorted to God, *"So do you think Job does all that out of the sheer goodness of his heart? Why, no one ever had it so good! You pamper him like a pet, make sure nothing bad ever happens to him or his family or his possessions, bless everything he does—he can't lose! But what do you think would happen if you reached down and took away everything that is his? He'd curse you right to your face, that's what"* (Job 1:9–11 MSG).

God's reply to Satan is interesting. Various Bible versions translate it differently, but in Job 1:12 from the *Good News Translation*, the Lord points out, *"Everything he has is in your power, but you must not hurt Job himself."* Satan left God's presence, and life was about to get bad for Job.

JOB 1:14–20 (AMP)
14 A messenger came to Job and said, "The oxen were plowing and the donkeys were feeding beside them,

15 and the Sabeans attacked *and* swooped down on them and took away the animals. They also killed the servants with the edge of the sword, and I alone have escaped to tell you."

16 While he was still speaking, another [messenger] also came and said, "The fire of God (lightning) has fallen from the heavens and has burned up the sheep and the servants and consumed them, and I alone have escaped to tell you."

17 While he was still speaking, another [messenger] also came and said, "The Chaldeans formed three bands and made a raid on the camels and have taken them away and have killed the servants with the edge of the sword, and I alone have escaped to tell you."

18 While he was still speaking, another [messenger] also came and said, "Your sons and your daughters were eating and drinking wine in their oldest brother's house,

19 and suddenly, a great wind came from across the desert, and struck the four corners of the house, and it fell on the young people and they died, and I alone have escaped to tell you."

20 Then Job got up and tore his robe and shaved his head [in mourning for the children], and he fell to the ground and worshiped [God].

Use your imagination and see this man Job. He just suffered a huge tragedy. What would you do? Would you fall to the ground and worship God? Or, would you blame Him? Verse 22 says Job did not sin by blaming God. Satan went back to the Lord and said, "He didn't curse You when he lost his possessions. But take away Your protection, and he'll curse you!" Again, God reminds Satan, *"He is in your power, but you are not to kill him"* (Job 2:6 GNT). This time Satan strikes Job with boils on his skin. He was in a sad condition as he sat in ashes, scraping his sores with broken pottery.

This is where many people equate themselves to Job. They are down in the dumps, nursing their wounds. Their lives are full of enormous difficulties and trouble. They have little and often lose what they do have. Some people call themselves "Job Junior"

The **Master Restorer:** God Will Do It Again

and wonder why bad things happen to them. Here is where understanding the truth about Job will help us.

There are many theories about how these things happened to Job and why God allowed Satan to do this. Remember, Satan is the god of this world (2 Cor. 4:4). He comes to steal, kill, and destroy whatever he can (John 10:10).

I believe Job opened the door of fear and allowed the enemy in. Satan could devour Job because he had already invited it through fear. As we study what happened to Job, we see that God put restraints on what the devil could do.

Job's Door of Fear

The Bible says Job's sons took turns having parties and feasts in their homes and invited their sisters. Job 1:5 (NLT) says, *"When these celebrations ended—sometimes after several days—Job would purify his children. He would get up early in the morning and offer a burnt offering for each of them. For Job said to himself, 'Perhaps my children have sinned and have cursed God in their hearts.' This was Job's regular practice."*

It doesn't say he offered sacrifices to God because they *had* sinned. He *feared* they *might have* sinned. We also see that this was his regular practice. Job allowed fear to rule him. After all those tragedies fell upon him, he said, *"What I always feared has happened to me. What I dreaded has come true"* (Job 3:25 NLT). Fear consumed Job! He lived in it daily. He was always afraid something terrible would happen. Fear unchecked will bring adverse consequences. Fear opens a door and allows Satan to destroy us!

We have a choice. We can be afraid, or we can be full of faith. Faith opens the door for God to continually bless us and keep us safe. We need to get a grip on fear and not allow it to get a hold on us!

The Master Restorer: God Will Do It Again

You can imagine how hard it was for Job when disaster struck. He also had no encouragement! His wife told him to curse God and die (Job 2:9). Then three friends came as comforters and stayed as tormentors (Job 2:11). For many chapters in the Book of Job, they kept telling him that everything happened because he sinned. Job constantly refuted their accusations, and scripture tells us he did not sin or blame God (Job 1:22; 2:10). He was wrongfully accused by even his friends.

Has someone ever visited you while you were facing a problem, and you felt worse after they left? Some people imply that everything happening to you is your fault. That's what Job's "comforters" told him.

But even during all the tragedy, Job showed signs of trusting in God. In Job 14:14 he asks, *"If a man dies, shall he live again? All the days of my hard service I will wait, till my change comes."* We can see here that Job expected change! And he declared that he would wait for it.

Restored Twice

Job asked an important question. All that Job had no longer existed. His family was gone. His possessions were gone. Then he lost his health. The situation seemed beyond repair. He was helpless. There was nothing but despair, and he cried out with the question of the age: Can something that is dead be made alive again?

The same question is asked today in one form or another. My marriage is dead. There is nothing left. Can it live again? My job is gone. Can my career live again? The doctor said I'm going to die. Can health thrive again? My life is shattered. Can it be restored? Can something that seems to be gone be revived?

The answer is yes. The first step is to close the door on fear and open the door of faith. If you trust God in faith, you expect something. Job admitted that he might have been down, but he confidently said, "My change is coming!" When Job spoke those words, he opened the door for God to

The **Master Restorer:** God Will Do It Again

come in and take control. In chapters 38–41, God confronted Job. He told him not to be presumptuous or fearful but to trust Him. Job repented and obeyed God, making changes based on what God said.

Whatever You Say

Remember, in Job's day there was no Bible. He couldn't turn to Psalm 34:19 and read, *"Many are the afflictions of the righteous, but the Lord delivers him out of them all."* He couldn't read what Paul wrote in Romans 8:37, *"Yet in all these things we are more than conquerors through Him who loved us."* Job lived long before Moses gave the law to the Israelites. Scholars consider this the oldest book in the Bible. The Bible didn't exist. It was just Job and God.

Today, when trouble comes, we have God's promises. We can resist fear by quoting the Word of God. One scripture everyone should learn and say often is Second Timothy 1:7: *"For God has not given us a spirit of fear, but of power and of love and of a sound mind."* When fear of any kind comes, fight it with this verse.

As I am confronted with the operation of a worldwide ministry, I have opportunities to quote that scripture several times a day. When situations and decisions reach my desk, there is nowhere else to go. So I go to God.

The other day, my wife, Lynette, said, "Look at this bill!" She is the chief financial officer of the ministry. We needed a lot of money to pay for something that had happened that week. Of course, the enemy repeated what he always says, "What are you going to do? You don't have the money." At times like that, if I allow fear to grip me, it will only bring destruction. Job said the thing he feared came upon him! I close the door to fear by saying, "I have not been given a spirit of fear, but of power, love, and a sound mind! My trust is in God. I will not let fear dominate me."

The Master Restorer: God Will Do It Again

Some people live with the same fear Job had—the fear of losing everything. The devil whispers, "What are you going to do?" They wring their hands and repeat, "Oh my, what am I going to do?" When the enemy brings circumstances to you and says, "You're going under," do you say, "Oh no! What's going to happen next?" I'll tell you what will happen—whatever you say! If you speak the Word, it will come to pass. If you lean into fear, then disaster is at your door.

Fear opens the door for bad things. If you have pain and think, "I have cancer," fear is ruling! You can resist fearful thoughts by quoting the Word. Express your faith by saying what the Bible says: "I have a sound body. I am healed by the power of God. Disease can't live in me in Jesus' Name."

Saying what the Bible says, shuts the door on fear. If you open it, you won't want to walk down that road! Job opened the door to disaster: *"What I fear most overtakes me. What I dread happens to me"* (Job 3:25 GW). But we can close the door to disaster with

Isaiah 54:17 and say, "No weapon formed against me will prosper!"

Choose to live in the promises of God. When fear threatens, say, "This is the day the Lord has made. All my needs are met according to His riches in glory. I overcome in Christ Jesus. Nothing that comes against me shall prosper!"

Forgiveness, Prayer, and Restoration

Throughout the Book of Job, you see that he never quit trusting God: *"Though He slay me, yet will I trust Him"* (Job 13:15). He didn't say, "Oh God, I lost everything!" No, he continued trusting God during his troubles.

When God spoke to Job (chapters 38–42), he realized he was in fear and changed. What happened as a result? Restoration! God restored *double*!

JOB 42:10 (NLT)
10 When Job prayed for his friends, the Lord restored his fortunes. In fact, the Lord gave him twice as much as before!

The Master Restorer: God Will Do It Again

Everything turned for Job when he prayed for his friends—the ones who told him all that junk! He quit thinking about himself and prayed for them. He is the one who trusted God—they were the ones who needed prayer.

In your darkest moments, praying for others with a genuine concern opens the door for God to move for you. Pray for the people who have said things against you. Stop being concerned about yourself and start being concerned about what happens to others. Things will turn around for you!

What did Jesus say? *"But I say to you, love your enemies, bless those who curse you, do good to those who hate you, and pray for those who spitefully use you and persecute you"* (Matt. 5:44). This happens regularly in the ministry. When it happens to me, I pray for them and say, "Lord, forgive them. They don't know what they're doing." As you intercede for those who have hurt you, God will move on your behalf.

Restored Twice

Don't try to fight those who oppose you. Some people can't seem to let it go when others talk about them. Who cares what they say? We must develop a thick-skinned attitude. What others think doesn't amount to anything. If we don't let it go, we can open the door for more junk to happen. Just pray for them, forget about it, and move on.

Now let's see what God did for Job. He didn't just restore him. *The Message* Bible says, *"After Job had interceded for his friends, God restored his fortune—and then doubled it!"* (Job 42:10 MSG). God restored to Job twice as much as he had before!

Satan tested Job, but Job didn't bow. He went through disaster, but he didn't quit trusting God. Likewise, the three Hebrew children went into the fiery furnace, but they didn't stop trusting God. Daniel went into the lion's den trusting God and came out unharmed. They all came out on the other side, and God restored them to a higher position!

The Master Restorer: God Will Do It Again

The same can happen to you if you trust God to turn your situation around. He is the master restorer, the turnaround specialist, and the God of more than enough! That's the way God does it—He always gives you more than you need! If we met Job after the last part of the book, we might think he never had any trouble. When God restores people, they look better than they did before!

People sometimes look at Kenneth Hagin Ministries today and think it's been an easy road. They weren't there when my dad started preaching faith and we were at rock bottom. They weren't there when I stood in my office window looking across the Rhema campus with the devil screaming, "What are you going to do now? How are you going to pay all these bills?" I took my Bible and put it on the floor. I literally stood on the Word of God and said, "God told us to start this school. I believe what He said. I'm going to keep standing on His Word." All those buildings and more are here today and paid for.

Restored Twice

In the middle of your worst nightmare, God will restore you in the same way He did Job. If He restored Job where he lived, He will restore you where you live. And you will be able to say, "Look at me now! Look at what God did!" Keep doing what God said to do no matter what anybody says. Keep trusting God no matter what anybody does. If God said it, believe it! That settles it. He is the restorer of the double!

Restoration in Action

Are you ready to change your life? This is your day! Close the door to fear and forgive those who hurt you. Even if your life is a mess, God can turn it into success! **Take another step of restoration and declare this:**

I resist fear and doubt in Jesus' Name. I choose to believe God and His Word. I will not be afraid. I will be strong and courageous. For God has not given me a spirit of fear, but of power, love, and a sound mind.

The Master Restorer: God Will Do It Again

Today I am choosing to love my enemies and pray for those who hurt, use, persecute, and hate me. Father, I forgive them. They do not know what they are doing. I will not repay evil for evil. I bless them. I do good to them. I pray that they may comprehend the love of Christ.

Thank you, Heavenly Father, for turning my captivity and restoring me. My change is coming! I'm ready to move forward!

Scriptures to Review

2 Chronicles 20:20

Psalm 56:3–4

Matthew 5:44

1 Peter 3:9

Ephesians 3:18

Deuteronomy 31:6

2 Timothy 1:7

Luke 23:34

Luke 6:27–28

4

Moving Forward

"Do not remember the former things, nor consider the things of old. Behold, I will do a new thing, now it shall spring forth; shall you not know it? I will even make a road in the wilderness and rivers in the desert."

—Isaiah 43:18–19

We have looked at the lives of Joseph and Job. Something to notice about them is they didn't let their past decide what God would do for them. Regardless of what happened, they trusted God. They weren't stuck in the glory days when life was good or when it was bad. They kept moving forward trusting God.

Too many people allow their past to dictate their future. Some don't think they deserve the good life God has for them.

The Master Restorer: God Will Do It Again

If that's you, forget about what took place and focus on what your Heavenly Father can do now! God's promises are the standard of His performance, not your past. It's not about what happened or what you did. It's about what God has done and His Word that is available to us. His promises assure us that He is *more* than enough!

ISAIAH 43:18–19 (MSG)
18 Forget about what's happened; don't keep going over old history.
19 Be alert, be present. I'm about to do something brand-new. It's bursting out! Don't you see it? There it is! I'm making a road through the desert, rivers in the badlands.

God spoke through Isaiah to Israel while they were in captivity in Babylon. They had disobeyed God by serving idols and removed themselves from God's protection. Then the Babylonians captured them, and they were forced to serve foreign masters. Their life was limited, and it looked as though they would be there forever.

Moving Forward

Bad things can happen when we don't obey God! But our Heavenly Father is not bringing adversity upon us. *We take* ourselves out from under His protection through disobedience. Bad things are always happening in the world. Living God's way and walking in obedience to His Word helps us stay under His protection.

When we experience affliction, we should do a personal checkup and see if we might not be coming in line with God. That's not always the reason for trials and tribulation. Human error or attacks from the enemy are also possibilities. But often our disobedience opens the door.

For many years, the Israelites lived under oppression, and the cause of it was their own doing. But God told them to forget about the former things—their past life, their limitations, and even their disobedience. That was yesterday, and they couldn't do anything about it. They had to forget what happened so that they could move forward with Him.

God was getting ready to do the impossible for the Israelites. They were about to be supernaturally set free! Their deliverance would be far beyond any human understanding or ability—something completely new. We can apply Isaiah 48:18–19 to our lives. We *must* learn to forget about the former things. It's the only way we can move forward with God.

Out With the Old

God's future for us is not based on our past—good or bad. Some people can't move forward because they keep remembering the sin and shame of former times. They still carry guilt. But God tells us to forget about that because He wants to do a new thing! Other people are hung up on the good experiences of their past—maybe things like Holy Ghost meetings they attended or experiences they had when they were first born again. But as long as they hang there, it is hard to go into the future with God!

Moving Forward

We cannot hold on to the past and move into something new with God. He has a wonderful future planned for us, but it is not based on what we have experienced. If we are holding on to something that happened before and want the same thing to happen again, we must let go. God wants to do new things!

Lot's wife is a good example of someone who clung to the old. *"But Lot's wife, from behind him, [foolishly, longingly] looked [back toward Sodom in an act of disobedience], and she became a pillar of salt"* (Gen. 19:26 AMP). When we don't let go of old things, we stop right there. We never advance into what God wants to do for us.

God wants to change our heart and thinking. He wants to give us a new vision. He wants to change our circumstances and our world! For that to happen, we must forget the past and allow God to bring the new.

This works both naturally and spiritually. We can get in a dilemma by preferring everything to be a certain way in church. If we always want a previous experience repeated, we get stuck there. God can't do anything new for us if we are always looking back.

Some people don't believe they can do anything for God *because* of their past. That's usually what is meant when we hear, "Let go of your past so you can move on with God!" But we also need to let go of past mountaintop experiences with God and allow Him to do something new.

The Spirit of God often moves like the waves of the sea. One wave rolls in, and we experience that for a while. Then another wave comes in. People can get stuck in one era and never move on. By doing so, they never get all that God wants for them. I've seen that happen all my life! And it's not just individuals. I have watched entire churches remain in one place because they wanted everything to stay the same.

Moving Forward

Let's make sure we are not living in the past so much that we aren't moving with God into the future. Let Him bring change! He is telling us, *"Be alert! I'm about to do something new!"* Our future is not based on our past. It's based on God's promises.

In With the New

When we are born again, we enter a new life, and a new future opens up for us. *"Therefore, if anyone is in Christ, he is a new creation; old things have passed away; behold, all things have become new"* (2 Cor. 5:17). *The Amplified Bible, Classic Edition* says: *"Therefore if any person is [ingrafted] in Christ (the Messiah) he is a new creation (a new creature altogether); the old [previous moral and spiritual condition] has passed away. Behold, the fresh and new has come!"*

Don't get hung up on previous spiritual conditions! It is easy to want the same spiritual experiences during a specific time in our lives or even a good service. I hear people say, "We had a Holy Ghost meeting last night!" I ask, "What about the night before? Wasn't the Holy Ghost there?" The general attitude is, "Oh yeah, I guess He was, but nothing happened."

To some people, it's not a Holy Ghost meeting unless you shout, dance, and run. But I have found that sometimes God speaks to people's hearts more in a quiet service than He does when there is a lot of activity! God wants us to have new experiences with Him. Don't get stuck in the same thing. Let's move with God into new areas!

When we became a new creation in Christ, we need to *stay* new! There are several TV programs where they turn old, ugly houses into new, beautiful homes. That's what God does with us when we're born again. He changes us. Then He wants to keep redoing that same "house" from the inside out!

As I mentioned in the Introduction, we are renovating Rhema Bible Church. Why? We're doing a new thing—the old needs to go! If we went back to what we did in the 1950s, people would leave. But changing the look of the platform or what we wear doesn't change the message!

Someone told me that the Holy Spirit couldn't move in my services because I don't wear a suit and tie. Since when did a suit determine how God moves? To reach a younger generation, we adopt new ways. Paul said, "I have become all things to all people so I might win some" (1 Cor. 9:19–23). Some people say you lose the Spirit when you bring fog and lights on the platform. But fog is just a water-based haze that makes the lights look pretty.

The message is still the same. Jesus saves. Jesus heals. And He is coming again! There is a Heaven to gain and a hell to shun. I preach just as well in a shirt, a pair of jeans, and boots as I do in a suit, tie, and alligator shoes!

God does not remain in the same place doing the same thing all the time. Yes, He is a God Who never changes (Num. 23:19), but He doesn't lead us the same way in every situation. The Apostle Paul tells us what attitude we need to have to follow God into new ways.

PHILIPPIANS 3:12–14

12 Not that I have already attained, or am already perfected; but I press on, that I may lay hold of that for which Christ Jesus has also laid hold of me.

13 Brethren, I do not count myself to have apprehended; but one thing I do, forgetting those things which are behind and reaching forward to those things which are ahead,

14 I press toward the goal for the prize of the upward call of God in Christ Jesus.

I like how *The Message Bible* translates these verses: *"I'm not saying that I have this all together, that I have it made. But I am well on my way, reaching out for Christ, who has so wondrously reached out for me. Friends, don't get me wrong: By no means do I count myself an expert in all of this, but I've got my eye on the goal, where God is beckoning us onward—to Jesus. I'm off and running, and I'm not turning back."*

Paul said this after many amazing things God did in and through him, even in great ministry crusades. He is echoing what Isaiah said. God wants us to move on to new things. Notice that Paul said, *"I press."* That means he had to put out some effort! If Paul had to press into the things of God, so should we!

There is more to be gained by pressing into what God has. No one has a corner on what God is doing. There is more revelation of His Word we can receive. There are more promises He wants us to possess. There is new fellowship God wants us to experience with Him. There is new territory to take. But we won't experience any of this by hanging back in the past.

I believe God wants to elevate us to a *new* level of faith so it can be said of us: *"Your faith groweth exceedingly"* (2 Thess. 1:3). Certainly, we thank the Lord for what has happened in the past! But every day is new in God. *This is the day the Lord has made.* We will rejoice and be glad in today, and we will go to the new heights with Him tomorrow!

Keeping In Step

In Isaiah 43:18–19, God didn't tell Israel what He was going to do. He said, "I'm going to do a new thing. Forget about what happened because I'm going to take you to a new place that is fresh and new!"

Spiritually, we need to keep in step with God and stay relevant to the things of God. Don't hang back from moving into new eras with Him. I'm not against the past. I'm not against shouting or dancing. I'm not against any of that! But if we stay there, we will miss the new God wants to do.

God does not want us to focus on our past life because He wants to bring us to a new life. Neither does He want us to be stuck on past spiritual experiences because He wants to bring us into new ones. When the new

Moving Forward

comes, we should say, "Here I am. I'm ready for the new thing. I don't know what it is, but I'm going to go with You!"

When I was a kid, I heard church people talk about how the Spirit of God moved back in the good old days. Then there was the Charismatic Renewal, and a lot happened through the Full Gospel Business Men's Fellowship. We crisscrossed the country preaching and teaching to crowds of five or six thousand! People were filled with the Holy Spirit, but there weren't churches for them to attend. That was then, and this is now. God wants to do something new!

At some point, we must focus on moving into the new. We must forget about the old things and press into all that God has for us.

We should never get tired of pressing! At times, we may want to relax, but there is no such thing. We must keep pushing forward!

It's like team sports. I have seen this happen in basketball and football games. One team may be ahead, but if they don't keep pushing, they lose the game. They relaxed because they had a big margin. But the next thing you know, the other team gains the momentum. They start scoring and win the game.

On the spiritual side, if we relax too much, the devil can gain momentum and blindside us before we figure out what took place. That happens when we quit pressing into the new things God has for us.

Be thankful for all of the great experiences with God. We needed them! They helped us at that time. But the great experiences of yesteryear will not help us today unless we allow them to propel us into the future. Dwelling on the past without pushing forward, won't help us to overcome. Let's press in with God and allow Him to do something new with our lives!

The new things may include some of the old, but God wants to take us to a place we have not been before. We will have the moving of the Spirit, but I don't know how it will

Moving Forward

come about. I have lived through many eras and moves of God. There has been a lull for a little while. I believe part of the reason is that people became satisfied with what they were doing. Let's get unsatisfied! Let's turn loose of the past. Let's go to the new era—because it is coming. A new revival is on the horizon. Are you ready to go with me? It's time!

Restoration in Action

It's time to change your world! The point we all need to get to is one of forgetting about our past great moments and opening up to what God wants us to move into. **Don't look back, and say this with me:**

I thank God for the new things!

I am determined to forget the past and reach for new revelation, new fellowship with God, new attitudes, new strength, new vision, and a new destiny!

I can't have what He has for me in the future until I turn loose of the past. I turn it loose today—good, bad, spiritual, everything!

The Master Restorer: God Will Do It Again

I wave goodbye to the past. I look forward and say hello to the future!

Old things are gone, and I press toward the new.

I will stay alert and be ready. Wherever you go, Holy Spirit, I will follow!

Thank You for leading me out of the past and into the future.

Scriptures to Review

Romans 6:4

Ephesians 4:22–24

2 Corinthians 5:17

John 16:13

Jeremiah 29:11

Psalm 23:3

Receive Jesus Today

If you have never accepted Jesus Christ as your personal Savior, you won't be able to enjoy the restoration described in this book. I want you to get in on it! And God does too. He wants to restore you in every way. The first step is accepting Jesus Christ as your personal Savior. He made it possible for you to come into a close relationship with God—born again spiritually into His family.

Consider the following scriptures, then pray the prayer below.

JOHN 6:37
37 All that the Father gives Me will come to Me, and the one who comes to Me I will by no means cast out.

The Master Restorer: God Will Do It Again

ROMANS 10:13

13 For "whoever calls on the name of the Lord shall be saved."

ROMANS 10:9–10

9 That if you confess with your mouth the Lord Jesus and believe in your heart that God has raised Him from the dead, you will be saved.

10 For with the heart one believes unto righteousness, and with the mouth confession is made unto salvation.

2 CORINTHIANS 5:21

21 For He made Him who knew no sin to be sin for us, that we might become the righteousness of God in Him.

Pray This

Heavenly Father, I come to You in the Name of Jesus. I know you will not cast me out, and I thank You for it. I believe in my heart that Jesus Christ is the Son of God. I believe He was raised from the dead to restore me to You. I confess Him now as my Lord. Thank You for making my life new

Receive Jesus Today

and giving me righteousness and salvation. I receive Your restoration in my life. Thank you for loving me. Thank you for turning my situations around. Today I have become Your child. Thank you for adopting me into the family of God. In Jesus' Name, I pray. Amen.

Signed_____

Date_____

If you prayed this prayer, I want to know about it! Email partnerservice@rhema.org or call 1-866-312-0972. I would like to help you start your Christian life with some free material. Congratulations on taking this important step, and welcome to the family of God! I am praying for you as you move forward with the master restorer.

Kenneth W. Hagin

"What should I do with my life?"

If you've been asking yourself this question, **RHEMA BIBLE TRAINING COLLEGE is a good place to come and find out.** RBTC will build a solid biblical foundation in you that will carry you through—wherever life takes you.

The Benefits:

- Training at *the* **top Spirit-filled Bible school**
- Teaching based on steadfast faith in God's Word
- Unique two-year core program specially designed to **grow** you as a believer, help you **recognize the voice of God**, and equip you to **live successfully**
- Optional **specialized training** in the third- and fourth-year program of your choice: Biblical Studies, Helps Ministry, Itinerant Ministry, Pastoral Ministry, Student Ministries, Worship, World Missions, and General Extended Studies
- **Accredited** with Transworld Accrediting Commission International
- Worldwide **ministry opportunities**— while you're in school

Apply today!
1-888-28-FAITH (1-888-283-2484)
rbtc.org

Rhema Bible Training College admits students of any race, color, or ethnic origin.

OFFER CODE—BKORD:PRMDRBTC

Rhema Word Partner Club

WORKING *together* TO REACH THE WORLD!

WPC

People. Power. Purpose.

Have you ever dropped a stone into water? Small waves rise up at the point of impact and travel in all directions. It's called a ripple effect. That's the kind of impact Christians are meant to have in this world—the kind of impact that the Rhema family is producing in the earth today.

The Rhema Word Partner Club links Christians with a shared interest in reaching people with the Gospel and the message of faith in God.

Together we are reaching across generations, cultures, and nations to spread the Good News of Jesus Christ to every corner of the earth.

To join us in reaching the world,
visit **rhema.org/wpc** or call **1-866-312-0972**.

Always on.

For the latest news and information on products, media, podcasts, study resources, and special offers, visit us online 24 hours a day.

rhema.org

Free Subscription!

Call now to receive a free subscription to *The Word of Faith* magazine from Kenneth Hagin Ministries. Receive encouragement and spiritual refreshment from . . .

- *Faith-building articles from Kenneth W. Hagin, Lynette Hagin, Craig W. Hagin, Denise Hagin Burns, and others*
- *"Timeless Teaching" from the archives of Kenneth E. Hagin*
- *Feature articles on prayer and healing*
- *Testimonies of salvation, healing, and deliverance*
- *Children's activity page*
- *Updates on Rhema Bible Training College, Rhema Bible Church, and other outreaches of Kenneth Hagin Ministries*

Subscribe today for your free *Word of Faith*!

1-888-28-FAITH (1-888-283-2484)

rhema.org/wof

OFFER CODE—BKORD:WF

Rhema
Correspondence Bible School

The Rhema Correspondence Bible School is a home Bible study course that can help you in your everyday life!

This course of study has been designed with you in mind, providing practical teaching on prayer, faith, healing, Spirit-led living, and much more to help you live a victorious Christian life!

Flexible
Enroll any time: choose your topic of study; study at your own pace!

Affordable

Profitable

"The Lord has blessed me through a Rhema Correspondence Bible School graduate.... He witnessed to me 15 years ago, and the Lord delivered me from drugs and alcohol. I was living on the streets and then in somebody's tool shed. Now I lead a victorious and blessed life! I now am a graduate of Rhema Correspondence Bible School too! I own a beautiful home. I have a beautiful wife and two children who also love the Lord. The Lord allows me to preach whenever my pastor is out of town. I am on the board of directors at my church and at the Christian school. Thank you, and God bless you and your ministry!"

—D.J., Lusby, Maryland

"Thank you for continually offering Rhema Correspondence Bible School. The eyes of my understanding have been enlightened greatly through the Word of God through having been enrolled in RCBS. My life has forever been changed."

—M.R., Princeton, N.C.

For enrollment information and a course listing, call today!

1-888-28-FAITH (1-888-283-2484)

rhema.org/rcbs

OFFER CODE—BKORD:BRCSC